The Wolf

by **Michael Dahl**

Reading Consultant:
Norm Bishop
Resources Interpreter
Yellowstone National Park

CAPSTONE BOOKS
an imprint of Capstone Press
Mankato, Minnesota

Capstone Books are published by Capstone Press
151 Good Counsel Drive, P.O. Box 669, Mankato, Minnesota 56002
http://www.capstone-press.com

Library of congress Cataloging-in-Publication Data
Dahl, Michael
    The wolf/by Michael Dahl
    p.cm.– (Wildlife of North America)
    Includes bibliographical references (p.45) and index.
    Summary: Details the characteristics, habitats, and life cycle of wolves.
ISBN 1-56065-471-6
    1. Wolves--North America--Juvenile literature. [1. Wolves.] I. Title. II. Series.
QL737.C22D34 1997
599.773'097--dc21

                      96-48683
                      CIP
                      AC

Photo credits
William Muñoz, 8, 12, 17, 20, 22, 23, 26, 28, 30,
    34, 38-39, 41, 43
Lynn M. Stone, cover, 6, 10, 14, 18, 24, 32

Table of Contents

Pronunciation guides follow difficult words, both in the text and in the
Words to Know section in the back of the book.

Fast Facts about Wolves

Scientific Name: Canis lupus; Canis rufus

Size: Wolves measure about five to six feet (about one and one-half to two meters) from the snout to the tip of the tail. They measure between two and three feet (60 and 90 centimeters) from the ground to the shoulder.

Weight: Adult wolves weigh between 50 and 150 pounds (between 22 and 68 kilograms).

Physical features: Wolves look like husky and malamute dogs. They have thick, shaggy fur and long bushy tails. They have strong legs, powerful jaws, and sharp teeth.

Color: Canis lupis is called the gray wolf. The gray is produced by a blend of colors. The colors are white, black, chestnut, and gray.

Life Span: Wolves generally live for nine or 10 years.

Habits: Wolves are social animals. They live and work together in groups called packs. Pack members protect each other and hunt and care for their young together.

Food: Wolves are predators. They hunt and eat other animals. Their food includes mice, rabbits, beavers, deer, and moose.

Reproduction: Mating occurs during the winter. The young are born in the spring. Females give birth to five or more pups at a time.

Range: Wolves live in North America, Europe, the Middle East, and Asia.

Habitat: Wolves live in forests, deserts, mountains, canyons, and swamps.

Chapter 1

The Wolf

A wolf is a wild dog. More than a dozen different kinds of wolves live in North America, Europe, the Middle East, and Asia. They can adapt to many climates. Wolves live in forests, deserts, mountains, canyons, and swamps.

Most wolves living in North America are gray wolves. They belong to a species called Canis lupus. A species is any group of living things with common characteristics. One small species of wolves exists in South Carolina and Texas. This species' scientific name is Canis rufus. These are red wolves.

Wolves are wild dogs that adapt to many climates.

Wolves living in warmer climates are smaller in size.

Gray wolves look like husky or malamute dogs. But they are larger than dogs. Gray wolves have longer legs, bigger feet, and narrower chests than dogs.

The average adult male wolf measures about five to six feet (about one and one-half to two meters) from the snout to the tip of the tail. Male wolves can weigh between 50 and 150 pounds (22 and 68 kilograms). The heaviest wolf on record weighed 170 pounds (76 kilograms).

Female wolves are generally smaller than males. They average four and one-half to six feet (about one to two meters) in length and weigh between 55 and 90 pounds (24 and 41 kilograms).

Adapting to Different Climates

The size and color of a wolf varies in different climates. Wolves living in the northern United States are larger than those living in the southern United States. Larger animals hold more body heat. Wolves living in colder climates have longer legs, bigger ears, and bigger bodies.

The color of a wolf's fur helps it blend into its surroundings. This helps wolves hide when hunting other animals. A gray wolf's coloring is a mixture of white, black, brown, and gray.

The color varies according to where the wolf lives. For example, wolves living in the Arctic are usually white. The white coat helps the wolf blend into the snow and surprise its prey. Prey are animals that wolves eat for food, such as rabbits, deer, and moose.

Chapter 2

Keen Hunters

Wolves are carnivores (KAR-nuh-vorz), which means they are meat eaters. An adult male can eat 20 pounds (nine kilograms) of meat in one kill. One kill is enough meat for 80 hamburgers.

Life in the wild is not easy. Although wolves are skillful hunters, they cannot always find prey. They often go hungry for weeks. Wolves prey on hooved animals such as moose, deer, caribou, musk-oxen, and elk. Sometimes it is difficult for wolves to catch a large animal. The hunt can last up to three hours.

Generally, wolves prefer to eat hooved animals. Red wolves are different. They live

Wolves can eat 20 pounds of meat in one meal.

where few hooved animals roam. They hunt small animals, such as mice, beavers, and rabbits. Gray wolves will also hunt small animals if they cannot kill a large one.

Wolves can hear the sound of rustling grass from thousands of feet (thousands of meters) away. A wolf's sharp eyesight can detect slight movements from one mile (1.6 kilometers) away. Its keen sense of smell can locate a moose two miles (three kilometers) away.

Hunting Together

Wolves can hunt alone, but they are pack animals. A pack is a group of animals that hunts and runs together. Wolves hunt more successfully in groups.

Wolves can only run 25 miles (40 kilometers) per hour for short distances. They can lope or jog seven and one-half miles (12 kilometers) per hour for 40 miles (64 kilometers). But hooved animals, such as the white-tailed deer, can run 40 miles (64 kilometers per hour. A white-tailed deer's speed makes it difficult to catch.

Wolves hunt in packs because it is easier to catch their prey.

A pack's size ranges from two to 20 members.

A pack ranges from two to 20 members, depending on the available food in a territory. A territory is a hunting area. An average pack's territory covers about 80 to 100 square miles (200 to 250 square kilometers). A pack will be small if few large, hooved animals live in its territory.

Packs mark their territory by urinating along the borders. Other packs smell the urine and do not hunt in this area.

Clever Hunters

Wolves approach a herd of animals from downwind. That way their prey cannot smell them. They creep forward and study their prey. Wolves kill mostly old, sick, or young animals. The weakest animals are easier to catch.

Wolves help keep other animal groups healthy. When wolves kill sick animals within a herd, it reduces the amount of disease. When they kill old animals, it increases the food supply for other animals. This helps to keep other animals in the herd healthy.

Generally, wolves chase their prey. They often watch to see which animal in a herd runs slower than the others. Then they will chase the animal until it is tired. When it is tired from running, it will have little chance of escaping.

Sometimes, however, the pack chooses its prey and stalks it. They surround the animal from a distance, so their prey cannot see them. Without being spotted, wolves can sneak within 30 feet (nine meters) of their prey. They continue moving closer to the animal until it notices them. Then the pack members stand still until their prey tries to escape.

Wolves then run after the animal and pull it down with their jaws. They rip and slash at its throat with their fangs. The throat of an animal bleeds easily. If the animal tries to run, it loses a lot of blood. Then the wolves kill the animal before it can get away. They rip it apart and eat most of the meat.

Wolves do not kill more than they need. If the pack cannot eat all of the meat at once, they will return to the kill until it is finished. Wolves do not waste any of their kill. Scavengers such as coyotes, ravens, and eagles feast on a pack's kill. After the meat is gone, wolves chew the bones to sharpen their teeth.

Wolves rip their prey apart and eat most of the meat.

Chapter 3

The Pack

A wolf pack follows a hierarchy (HYE-er-ar-ke). This is a rank within the pack. Some wolves are leaders while others are followers. The two leading wolves are called the alpha male and alpha female.

Alpha wolves are the strongest and most experienced hunters. They direct the pack's actions and keep it under control. Alpha wolves are always the first to eat after a kill.

The next-highest ranking wolves are the beta male and beta female. Sometimes the beta male mates with the alpha female. This

The alpha male and alpha female are leaders of the pack.

happens when the alpha male does not want to mate. Omega wolves follow the beta wolves in rank.

The lowest ranking wolves are peripheral (puh-RIF-ur-uhl) wolves. These wolves are often lone wolves trying to join a pack. They have no rank and eat last.

When a wolf leaves a pack, it becomes a lone wolf. This may happen if an omega wolf leaves the pack. An alpha wolf forced out of its lead position also sometimes leaves the pack. A lone male wolf will try to find a lone female wolf to start its own pack.

Structure Changes

The social structure of the pack changes to fit its needs. As alpha wolves grow older, they may become weaker than other pack members. Then the pack needs a change in leadership. A change in leadership may be a peaceful or violent situation.

Sometimes a beta wolf challenges an alpha wolf to a fight. The wolf that wins the fight

Lone wolves try to find a pack that will accept them.

proves its strength and dominance. The winning wolf takes charge and leads the pack.

Rank Is Important

When two wolves meet, their body language shows their rank. The higher-ranking wolf commands respect. It will stand tall, with its ears erect, and its tail held straight out. It will stretch up on its legs and walk stiffly.

The lower-ranking wolf bows its head and lies down. When a lower-ranking wolf lies down, it shows its belly. This is a sign of weakness. After this greeting, the two wolves know their standing in the pack. Then they wag their tails, play, and hunt.

WOLF TRACKS

Front Foot   Back Foot

A lower-ranking wolf shows its belly as a sign of weakness.

Chapter 4

The Wolf Family

Wolves try to mate for life. If their mate dies, they may mate with another wolf. The alpha female controls the amount of mating in the pack. Usually only the alpha female mates with either the alpha or beta male. Generally, the alpha female mates with the alpha male. If lower omega wolves try to mate, the alpha wolves usually stop them.

The alpha male and female have a close relationship during the year. This relationship grows closer before the mating period. The

The alpha male and alpha female are mates for life.

alpha male and female stay close to each other. The alpha female mates with the alpha male wolf several times. Pups are born about 63 days later.

Mating takes place during the late winter months from January to April. Mating in late winter gives pups born in spring time to become strong before winter.

Preparing a Home

A few weeks before the pups are born, the mother selects a den. The den is a cave or a hole in the ground. A den may be created in a hollow log or in an old beaver house.

The father helps prepare for the newborn pups. He will find meat and store it for the mother. She does not like to leave her pups after they are born. He brings pieces of his fresh kill and buries them near the den.

Female wolves usually have five or six pups in a litter. A litter is a group of pups born at the same time to one mother. Litters may have as few as one and as many as 10 pups. The average weight of a pup is one pound (one-half kilogram) at birth.

Wolves open their eyes within two weeks of birth. When the pups are three weeks old, they can hear, and they can eat solid food.

Pups Learn and Grow

The mother and other pack members feed the pups warm meat. The pups' meat is half-digested. The mother wolf swallows the meat first. Then she brings the meat back up for the pups to eat. Pups also depend on other pack members to spit up food for them.

Wolf pups play to develop their strength and hunting skills.

Every pack member helps take care of the pups. Pack members baby-sit and feed the litter. When pack members go out on a hunt, one adult stays with the pups. Pack members return from the hunt with fresh meat to feed the litter.

Pups learn to hunt by playing. They run, chase, pounce, and fight. This helps them develop their strength and hunting skills. Pups learn to trust and depend on other pack members. This closeness also helps pups understand their own rank in the pack.

The Rendezvous Site

When pups are one month old, they begin to leave the den. The pack moves to a new place. This place is called a rendezvous (RON-day-voo). A rendezvous is a resting spot in grassy countryside surrounded by forest. Here the pups learn the ways of an adult wolf.

The wolves stay at the rendezvous site through summer. By late September or early October, the pups are big enough to hunt with the pack. The pups learn their hunting skills from older pack members.

Scat, pictured below, is used to find out where an animal lives and what it eats.

The pups cannot leave the pack until they are two years old. At the age of two, they are considered adults.

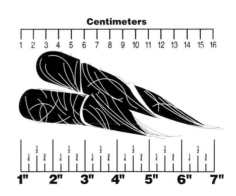

Centimeters

1 2 3 4 5 6 7 8 9 10 11 12 13 14 15 16

1" 2" 3" 4" 5" 6" 7"

Chapter 5

The Future of Wolves

Some people admire wolves while others fear them. Some of the early North American settlers hated wolves. The wolves killed their livestock, so settlers started to kill them. But the wolf was respected by many North American Indians. In many of their legends, the wolf played the role of the teacher.

Pawnee Creation Legend

The wolf plays a role in a Pawnee Indian legend about how the earth was made. The

Wolves are both feared and admired.

Pawnee are Plains Indians who once lived in what is now Nebraska and Wyoming. This story comes from the book *Of Wolves and Men* by Barry Holstun Lopez.

All the animals met to decide how to make the earth. Everyone was invited except the brightest star in the southern sky, the Wolf Star. The Wolf Star became angry about being left out.

The animals told the Storm that Comes out of the West to travel around the earth. He made sure that the creation went well. The Storm carried a bag with him. The bag contained the earth's first people. When the Storm stopped at night, he let the people out of the bag. They camped and hunted buffalo.

The Wolf Star sent a gray wolf to follow the Storm. When the Storm fell asleep, the wolf stole his bag. The wolf thought there was something to eat inside. When he opened the bag, the people came out. They set up camp, but they could not find buffalo to hunt. They realized that the wolf had let them out of the

The Wolf Star sent a gray wolf to follow the Storm.

bag, not the Storm. They became angry and killed the wolf.

When the Storm saw what the people had done, he became sad. He told them that by killing the wolf, they let death into the world. This was not the plan, but now it was this way.

The Storm told the people to make a sacred bundle out of the wolf's skin. Inside, they put things that reminded them of what happened. The Storm said they would be known as the wolf people, the Skidi Pawnee.

The Wolf Star watched all of this. The Pawnee call this star Fools the Wolves. This star rises just before the morning star. It tricks wolves into howling before it is light. In this way, the Wolf Star reminds us that he was forgotten during the creation of the earth.

An Endangered Species

Today, wolves are an endangered species. An endangered species is any group of animals in danger of dying off. Several recovery programs have started in the United States. Recovery programs capture endangered wild animals and

The star called Fools the Wolves rises before morning and tricks wolves into howling.

Where the Wolf lives

release them into protected areas. Protected areas are parks where people may not hunt or harm animals.

The gray wolf once lived in Yellowstone National Park in Wyoming. But wolves have not lived in that park for more than 60 years.

The wolves were hunted and killed. People wanted to enjoy the elk and deer.

But over the years, people felt that the elk and deer population grew too large. It also seemed there was not enough food. People were afraid that elk and deer would damage young trees.

Today, Yellowstone National Park is bringing the wolf back to its natural habitat. In January 1995, 14 gray wolves were captured from four packs in Alberta, Canada. They were brought to Yellowstone and held in pens for nine weeks. Then they were released. The wolves produced two litters for a total of nine pups.

In 1996, the wolves had four litters with a total of 14 pups. Eleven wolves have died since their release. The Yellowstone recovery program has increased the population of gray wolves to 52. The program seems to be a success.

Some people feel that gray wolves should not be reintroduced into Yellowstone National Park. Ranchers and farmers living near the park fear that wolves will kill their livestock.

Defenders of Wildlife is an organization that prevents the illegal killing of wolves by paying

Snout

Paw

White Underbelly

Shaggy Fur

Hind Leg

Long Tail

ranchers for any loss of livestock. Defenders of Wildlife also hopes to provide ranchers with guard dogs that will protect livestock without killing wolves.

Red Wolves

In 1975, scientists thought 100 red wolves lived on the coast of Texas. Scientists studied the wolves. But they found that most of these animals were part coyote and not red wolves. The scientists only found 10 pure red wolves. These red wolves were caught and placed on a farm in Washington. There, scientists bred the wolves and studied them.

By 1978, the population had increased to 50 red wolves. These wolves were placed in different parts of the country. Otherwise, a sickness on one farm could kill the whole population. In 1978, scientists finally set two red wolves into the wild.

The scientists still had to help red wolves live in the wild. They helped sick wolves recover and made sure the wolves stayed in a safe area. The first pair of red wolf pups were born in the wild

In 1975, scientists found only 10 pure red wolves.

in the 1990s. Today about 500 red wolves live in South Carolina and Texas on farms or ranches.

Helping the Wolves

Today, wolves are still being hunted. In Minnesota, wolves are killed illegally every year. Concerned people can help the wolves.

There are several conservation groups that enlist the help of volunteers. Many of these conservation groups lobby for animal and wolf rights. Lobbying means asking public officials to create laws that protect animals.

Concerned people can help wolves by adopting them. Some conservation groups have a program where a person can pay a yearly fee to adopt a wolf. This money is used for projects and research to protect wolves. The person adopting the wolf receives a photo, a certificate, and a name for the wolf. If many people become involved, scientists have a better chance of saving the wolf.

People can help save wolves by getting involved with a conservation group.

Words to Know

carnivore (KAR-nuh-vor)—an animal that eats meat

dominant (DOM-uh-nuhnt)—something or someone with more power

endangered species (en-DAYN-jured SPEE-seez)—a species in danger of dying out

livestock (LIVE-stok)—domestic animals raised by ranchers and farmers

pack (PAK)—a group of animals that hunts and lives together

peripheral (puh-RIF-ur-uhl)—the outer edge

predator (PRED-uh-tur)—an animal that eats other animals to survive

prey (PRAY)—animals that other animals eat

rendezvous (RON-day-voo)—a spot where cubs stay during the pack's hunt

scat (SKAT)—animal droppings

territory (TER-uh-tor-ee)—an area where animals hunt and roam

To Learn More

Parker, Barbara Keevil. *North American Wolves.* Nature Watch. Minneapolis: Carolrhoda Books, 1998.

Patent, Dorothy Hinshaw. *Gray Wolf, Red Wolf.* New York: Clarion Books, 1994.

Smith, Roland. *Journey of the Red Wolf.* New York: Cobblehill Books, 1996.

Weide, Bruce and Patricia Tucker. *There Is a Wolf in the Classroom!* Minneapolis: Carolrhoda Books, 1995.

Zeaman, John. *How the Wolf Became the Dog.* Before They Were Pets. New York: Franklin Watts, 1998.

Useful Addresses

Canadian Wolf Defenders
P.O. Box 3480, Station D
Edmonton, AB T5L 4J3
Canada

Defenders of Wildlife
1101 Fourteenth Street NW
Suite 1400
Washington, DC 20005

H.O.W.L. (Help Our Wolves Live)
4600 Emerson Avenue South
Minneapolis, MN 55409

International Wolf Center
1396 Highway 169
Ely, MN 55731

Internet Sites

Canadian Centre for Wolf Research
http://www.wolfca.com

North American Wolf Assocation
http://www.nawa.org

Nova Online—Wild Wolves
http://www.pbs.org/wgbh/nova/wolves

Powerful Symbols
http://www.powersource.com/gallery/objects/
    default.html

What Is a Wolf?
http://www.wolfhaven.org/whatisa.htm

Index